ABBA
&
MAMMA MIA

Written by Claire Welch

ABBA
&
MAMMA MIA

This edition first published in the UK in 2007
by Green Umbrella Publishing

© Green Umbrella Publishing 2008

www.gupublishing.co.uk

Publishers Jules Gammond & Vanessa Gardner

Printed and bound in Italy

ISBN 978-1-906635-72-5

Contents

Introduction

Introduction

RIGHT Introducing ABBA, 1974

ABBA-MANIA FIRST TOOK ON A global dimension on 6 April 1974 when the Swedish pop group consisting of Benny Andersson, Björn Ulvaeus, Agnetha Fältskog and Anni-Frid Lyngstad won the Eurovision Song Contest in Brighton. "Waterloo" was the song that was to launch their international career when they won that night with its catchy tune, European flavour and universal lyrics. But, it wasn't just the catchy song, good looks of the band members, outlandish costumes (which still seem to be a strong theme with Eurovision today) and the love interest between the singers that were to win through, it was the sheer determination of manager Stig Anderson that was to set ABBA on the road to fame and international stardom.

It all began for ABBA in June 1966 when Björn and Benny met at a party. Björn was a member of the Hootenanny Singers while Benny was an up and coming performer with the Hep Stars. The Hootenanny Singers were a studio based group who released their records on Polar Music, formed and owned by Stig Anderson and his long-time friend Bengt Bernhag. Both Björn and Benny were already successful musicians in their own right, but with Stig Anderson's help they were about to conquer the world. But a songwriting duo – who co-wrote their first song in 1966 – weren't about to do it on their own.

RIGHT Agnetha in bed with a cold, comforted by Björn

Both men met their future partners – both professionally and personally – in the spring of 1969. Benny met Anni-Frid (Frida) while both were performing in a Swedish festival and Björn met Agnetha. Both women were about to become their fiancées and the other all important half of their phenomenal pop group.

Agnetha and Björn married in 1971,

but Benny and Frida managed to wait another seven years before they tied the knot. In the beginning, ABBA didn't exist in the way that the world would see them. The four collaborated on songs written by Benny and Björn while Agnetha and Frida contributed backing vocals. Stig Anderson was often instrumental in the lyrics – something he was already renowned for in Sweden – and many of the first songs that transpired from the group were solos or duets.

The group became known as Festfolk and their first medium-sized hit came in 1972 with "People Need Love". It was the first time that the two women had provided the lead vocals and all four members of the band – along with manager Anderson – realised that here they might just have a winning formula. Encouraged somewhat by their success, the band entered the Swedish heats of the Eurovision Song Contest in 1973 with "Ring Ring". Although it lacked the feisty-style that was to come it did encourage some attention to the band in other European countries. They were particularly popular in Sweden. However, it did not do what Stig Anderson wanted and take them to the Eurovision Song Contest. In fact, the song trailed in third place and all four band members were deeply disappointed.

When Stig Anderson got fed up with naming all four band members every time he gave an interview or promoted the band in any other way he decided to change their name to ABBA – an acronym of all four members' first initials. It worked and the name stuck. It was far more practical, buzzing and contemporary than any band name they had had before. After winning the Eurovision Song Contest in 1974, ABBA would have a huge hit with "Waterloo" hitting the hot spot in the charts all over Europe – although strangely, it never made it to Number 1 in the US. The group's first album following their success in Brighton was cannily also

called "Waterloo" and went on to become a huge hit in Sweden.

However, despite coming to international attention by winning Eurovision, the success of that night also had its drawbacks. Eurovision was openly referred to as "a joke" by many of ABBA's would-be audiences and it was to prove difficult for the group to be taken seriously at first. It would take ABBA another 18 months before the world at large really began to sit up and take notice. The third album, "ABBA" seemed to be the key with its hugely successful number "SOS". Another song from the album, "Mamma Mia", saw ABBA take the hot spot in the UK and Australia. The group from the cold northern hemisphere country with little daylight were about to create ABBA fever in one of the hottest and sunniest countries on the planet. The Australians absolutely loved ABBA. They went wild for them and ABBA fever basically shook Australia for six years.

By 1976, ABBA was firmly established as one of the most popular groups in the world. The same year saw the group release different greatest hits compilations in both the UK and Australia; in the UK it was "ABBA's Greatest Hits"

RIGHT Smiles and
sunglasses, 1976

while in Australia they released "The Best Of ABBA". "Fernando" and "Dancing Queen" – the latter with lyrics by Stig Anderson – both topped the charts in many countries across the globe and in April 1977, "Dancing Queen" became the group's only US Number 1. A fourth album, "Arrival", was aptly named in 1976 as it neatly coincided with the group's dominance on the world stage. Proving just how popular ABBA were, the album stormed up the charts with hits including "Money, Money, Money" and "Knowing Me, Knowing You".

Next for ABBA came a successful tour of Europe and Australia in 1977 which played to sell-out venues with scream-ing audiences – which would bother Agnetha – at every concert they gave. It was also the year when ABBA began work on a feature film, *ABBA – The Movie*, which premiered in December 1977 to coincide with the release of a fifth album, "ABBA – The Album". Memorable numbers from the album included "Take A Chance On Me" and "The Name Of The Game".

The following year saw ABBA take to the stage in the US where they reached Number 3 with "Take A Chance On Me"

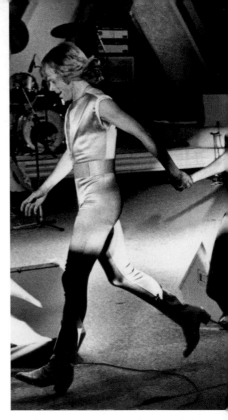

and made it into the Top 20 album charts with "ABBA – The Album". The singles "Chiquitita" and "Summer Night City" were followed by "Voulez-Vous", the band's sixth album which was released in April 1979. But all was not well for Björn and Agnetha who had previously announced their impending divorce although both had agreed to stay with ABBA. This didn't help the image that the band had of two loving couples happily making music to a worldwide audience.

In 1979, "Gimme! Gimme! Gimme!" was released in the autumn and was then immediately followed by a major tour in Canada, the US and Europe. The second compilation album was also released around this time and once again proved to be a massive hit for the group. In March 1980, the group toured Japan and followed this by recording their next album "Super Trouper" with the title track and "The Winner Takes it All" reaping success.

The following year it looked as if ABBA were headed for a downward spiral as Benny and Frida announced that they too would be heading for a divorce. Despite the emotional turmoil going on within the band, the four members still worked together and "The Visitors" – their eighth album – was released. "One Of Us" taken from the album proved to be a huge hit but the strain of working with ex-partners was, by now, taking its toll.

In 1982, Benny and Björn announced that they would be concentrating their

efforts on writing their new musical, Chess, in collaboration with Sir Tim Rice. Stig Anderson firmly believed that they would be back, but he was to be proved wrong. Agnetha and Frida were pursuing solo careers and it looked unlikely that ABBA, as it had been, would ever be the same again. The group released "The Singles – The First Ten Years" and then decided to take a "break". It has turned out to be the longest "break" in history and today, fans, music critics and the world at large recognise the fact that ABBA are extremely unlikely to perform together again.

Chapter 1

Formation

RIGHT Relaxed in the '70s

WHEN FRIDA RECORDED "PETER Pan" – co-written by Benny and Björn – in 1969 it was to bring together the first three members of the band that were to become known as ABBA. Benny provided the keyboards on the original recording and Stig Anderson, who had already provided lyrics for Frida's solo career, was hovering in the background. The collaboration between Benny, Björn, Frida and Anderson was already well under way. Then came Agnetha and the four musicians began working on an album for a cabaret show called Festfolket. They gave their first performance together on a Swedish radio show Våra Favoriter on 3 October 1970 that also featured the artists performing their own songs as well.

The cabaret show went on tour across Sweden in early 1971 but the two couples almost ended their collaboration there and then. It was not a happy experience for the four musicians who found the tour gruelling and exhausting. Any plans they may have had to work together as a foursome were quickly fading and Frida left the three other members of the group to go on tour with Lars Berghagen, the Swedish singer and songwriter with whom she already had an established professional relationship. A

RIGHT At the airport,
1974

RIGHT At the airport,
1974

duet by Frida and Berghagen
entered the Swedish charts and
was quite successful.

Although plans to work together
as a foursome had been shelved,
Benny, Björn, Agnetha and Frida
still worked on each others' recordings. The first time they recorded
together was when Agnetha and
Frida provided the backing vocals
for Benny and Björn's album "Hej
Gamle Man!" And when Frida
went on to release her first chart-
topper in 1971 with "Min Egen
Stad", the backing vocals were provided by Benny, Björn and
Agnetha. Between the end of 1971
and the early part of 1972, collaboration between the four musicians
began to grow. It was fitting that
Frida's last solo single for EMI
included an A-side written by
Benny and Björn with lyrics on the
B-side provided by Stig Anderson.
Benny produced the single and was
a backing vocalist along with Björn
and Agnetha. From then on in, the
four of them began to work
together regularly and their time
on the world stage was about to
begin in the guise of ABBA.

Chapter 2

Fame and The Eurovision Song Contest

STIG ANDERSON WAS INSTRUMENtal in ABBA's success at the Eurovision Song Contest in 1974. Anderson had prepared the group meticulously for the event and he saw Eurovision as the key to ABBA's breakthrough in the international arena. It may have been unheard of for a Swedish group to win the contest, but Anderson believed that he, and ABBA, had the recipe for success. He had four great looking performers who were all close friends and there was also the love interest in that the band was formed of two couples. At this point,

Björn and Agnetha were parents to one-year-old Linda. They also had a magical appeal with their harmonious and instantly "feel-good" music which combined with their glitzy costumes – gave them glamour and sparkle. The early 1970s were full of artists in outlandish gear including Gary Glitter, David Bowie, the Bay City Rollers, Elton John and Alvin Stardust to name but a few.

Although there was some feeling –

and still is – that Eurovision was fun and a bit of a joke and not something that everyone takes that seriously, Anderson was convinced that it was the right vehicle to promote his energetic group. Despite its reputation, the con-

test had proved time and again that any winning song would be instantly propelled to the top of the European charts while the winning performers would become overnight stars. The year before, ABBA had entered the Swedish

RIGHT ABBA meeting
at Waterloo

RIGHT ABBA meeting
at Waterloo

finals for Eurovision with the already mentioned "Ring Ring" which had brought them instant success at home. There was a national outcry when the band was not selected by a panel of judges and the young and talented singer, Lena Anderson, was sent to represent Sweden instead. Such was the furore that followed that the selection process for 1974 was changed so that ABBA could take the competition by storm. The major factor that gave ABBA a landslide victory over their other competitors was that the Swedish public were allowed to vote for the act that they deemed most likely to win Eurovision. As with "Ring Ring" the previous year, "Waterloo" was deemed by the Swedish public to have what it would take.

"Waterloo", originally entitled "Honey Pie", was the song that the Swedish public wanted the rest of Europe to hear. The press – who couldn't get enough of the group – also added to the hype and ABBA became a domestic phenomenon with Stig Anderson, the exceptional entrepreneur, keeping the bandwagon rolling. "Waterloo" went on to top the Scandinavian charts and Anderson began his campaign further afield in other European countries

RIGHT Happy in the park after Eurovision success

including Denmark where the group became particularly popular. Demo tapes were sent wherever possible to sway opinion on the forthcoming contest while Anderson released pictures of the band as far and as wide as possible. There are even some documentaries that claim that stickers with the word "Waterloo" also appeared in various places – including Brighton – where the contest would be held. On the day of the 1974 Eurovision, ABBA stickers were apparently everywhere. The result was that people began to take this little-known Swedish band seriously.

The title of the song was eventually chosen by Stig Anderson who had predicted that a catchy name would do wonders. "Honey Pie" had been abandoned in favour of his preferred choice "Waterloo" which Anderson and the band felt had a European flavour – although there were some concerns over which way the French voting would go – and the song had some relevance to a large audience across the continent.

"Waterloo" had taken time to materialise. Anderson, Benny and Björn had spent many hours working on the number to ensure that it was exactly

right for the voting countries across Europe. On 6 April 1974, ABBA found themselves up against Olivia Newton-John, representing the UK with "Long Live Love", Anne-Karine Strom from Norway, Holland's Mouth & McNeal and Irene Sheer, representing the previous year's winning country Luxembourg – a country who were loath to win again because they cited that they couldn't afford to host yet another Eurovision. However, the bookies' original quote of 20-1 for ABBA to win started to fall as the mood veered towards the Swedish group, despite Olivia Newton-John's popularity as the 7-2 favourite. In addition, Ireland was also a popular choice with their performer, Tina, and her song "Cross Your Heart".

The Brighton Dome in the rain-swept south east was the venue that was set to host the competition that night and the band were understandably nervous. This was their chance to make the big time and an entire nation was expecting them to achieve the almost unthinkable – to win. Agnetha had literally been sewn into her costume and she was feeling uncomfortable and perhaps, a little bit vulnerable. The live show, with

its 17 competitors was watched by more than 500 million people in 32 countries. ABBA's conductor was Sven-Olof Waldoff who was dressed like Napoleon Bonaparte – unusual for a conductor who was usually seen in tails – and ABBA were dressed in tight-fitting costumes which left little to the imagination. Indeed, Agnetha's costume was to start a worldwide fascination with her bottom which would last throughout her career! With hosts, Katie Boyle and Terry Wogan, ABBA took to the Brighton stage and prepared to set the world, let alone Europe, alight.

As soon as Waldoff brought his baton into play ABBA gave the live audience the performance they wanted to hear. It was clear to all concerned that there was no contest between the band from

Sweden and the other competitors. ABBA gave an outstanding performance which brought the house down. The song was an instant success with its bouncy catchiness. In a split second, the drabness of the previous acts was obliterated by this Scandinavian sensation. With the subsequent other acts over, the scores quickly began to tell their own story. A landslide victory was clearly theirs. The elation for the four band members, Anderson and Waldoff was watched by millions before ABBA jumped onto the stage for the finale. "Waterloo" had provided a fresh approach to Eurovision that was much needed and longed for by the organisers and fans alike. No wonder it won by a landslide victory.

Following the after-show party and the celebrations back at the hotel which included drinking copious amounts of champagne, the reality started to sink in when "Waterloo" went on to take the Number 1 spot at the top of the pop charts across the globe. It would mean that ABBA would be forever linked with Eurovision, but at that time the band didn't care. It was what they had worked for, what they had strived for – this instant stardom on an international

break some 10 years later.

It could also be that, despite their popular appeal, their music didn't attract a serious audience because it was quite simply pop music. It was fresh, it was lively, the performers were energetic with outlandish costumes and the music that the band cultivated didn't try to be something it wasn't. ABBA was happy to be performing pop music – it's what they did best. They had a unique style, they weren't dressing their music up as anything else and it had universal appeal (although they themselves were dressing up in costumes that had the media and fans alike in turmoil). With instantly memorable choruses, some moving soulful ballads and clever harmonies mixed with exciting rhythms, ABBA

playing field. But whether it was Eurovision, or whether it was the fact that they were Swedish, ABBA's music was never taken seriously from the moment they won right up until they announced they were taking a ensured themselves of success and became the top pop band of the 1970s and 1980s, while Benny and Björn would prove without a doubt they were the greatest songwriters of the 20th century.

Chapter 3

Benny Andersson

THE EXCEPTIONAL MUSICIAN Göran Bror Benny Andersson was born in Stockholm in Sweden on 16 December 1946. The composer and performer has enjoyed a remarkable career since he joined the Swedish group the Hep Stars. His father, Gösta Andersson, was a construction worker and Benny had a younger sister, Eva-Lis, who was born two years after him in 1948. Both his father and grandfather were musical and played the accordion and presented the young Benny, then aged six, with his own instrument. He learnt Swedish folk music – taught by both his father and grandfather – as well as traditional music. But he was heavily influenced by the "King" of rock and roll, Elvis Presley.

Aged 10, he taught himself to play the piano and when he left school at 15 he began performing in youth clubs where

he met Christina Grönvall. The couple had two children, Peter (born 1963) and Helen (born 1965). Benny and Christina joined the Electricity Board Folk Music Group in 1964 where the music consisted mainly of instrumentals including the number "Baby Elephant Walk" written by Benny.

It was around this time that he began writing his own songs which the band were more than happy to perform. The group found themselves up against the Hep Stars in a talent contest in March 1964 and Benny took over as the competitors' keyboard player later that year. Playing for the Hep Stars, he realised that he wanted a career as a professional musician.

Benny didn't have to wait long for a taste of success with his new band. Their breakthrough came in March 1965 with

the group's hit "Cadillac". It was to lead to a successful career and the Hep Stars were to become one of Sweden's most celebrated pop bands during the 1960s. Benny found himself a driving force for the band using his own

"Sunny Girl", "She Will Love You" and "It's Nice To Be Back" to name but a few. But, despite Benny's songwriting abilities the band also continued to perform cover versions of many international hits as these gave them more of a following.

It was probably Benny's chance meeting with the Hootenanny Singers on a road just outside Ålleberg while travelling with the Hep Stars that was to change his fortunes forever. The Hep Stars were invited to a party later that night and it was here that Benny was to meet Björn Ulvaeus. The year was 1966 and after a successful party – where both bands played songs by the Beatles – Benny and Björn found that they were ideally suited to working together. Their first collaboration was "Isn't It Easy To Say" which the Hep Stars recorded. But Björn wasn't the only musician with whom Benny was working.

He had an established writing partnership with Lasse Berghagen and the two songwriters wrote a number of popular numbers together including "Hey, Clown" for the Swedish Eurovision Song Festival. The song made it to the finals of the competition in 1969 and finished in second place.

LEFT ABBA taking a chance

material which proved popular with the band's fans including hits such as "No Response", "Wedding", "Consolation",

The festival, however, wasn't just going to prove successful musically, it was to prove successful on a personal level too. At the festival, Benny met Anni-Frid Lyngstad who was also participating in the festival and they soon became a couple. At around the same time, Björn met Agnetha. The four friends then became very close as their friendships blossomed and their music looked as if it could reach the big time with Benny's and Björn's continued writing collaboration. "Ljuva Sextiotal" and "Speleman" were hits for Brita Borg and the Hep Stars respectively but the voices of Agnetha and Anni-Frid (Frida) were beginning to convince Benny and Björn that their own group could follow in the footsteps of acts such as the Sweet and Blue Mink among others. ABBA was a fledgling band that was about to take the world by storm.

Benny enjoyed 11 successful years with ABBA before the foursome split in 1982.

The ABBA years resulted in seven studio albums, global success and a run of Number 1 hits. But, following the decline of ABBA, his career was far from over, despite the lack of outlandish costumes. Even though Benny and Björn were unable to read music, the partnership between them continued and further collaboration saw the musical, Chess, unleashed in front of both a London and a Broadway audience. The show was well-received in London, but suffered a fair amount of criticism in New York. The album of music from Chess was released in 1984 with vocals by Elaine Paige, Barbra Dickson – including "I Know Him So Well" – Murray Head, Tommy Körberg and Björn Skifswas. The album was a huge success and sold more than two million copies worldwide. "I Know Him So Well" became a huge Number 1 hit and "One Night In Bangkok" sung by Murray Head made it to Number 3 in the US charts. The Prince Edward Theatre in London's West End was home to the musical for three years between May 1986 and 1989. But when the show opened on Broadway in 1988, despite two successful years in London, it was panned by the critics on the other side of the Atlantic and closed after only two months.

Meanwhile, Benny produced and released an album in 1985 with Swedish vocalists, Anders and Karin Glenmark (a brother and sister duo who had added many vocals to recordings on Chess). The Benny and Björn collaboration was as strong as ever and named Gemini, the Glenmarks released a second collaboration in 1987 with Benny and Björn, their old friends. One of the biggest hits to come out of the album was "Mio My Mio". The same year would also see Benny release his first solo album "Chime, My Bells" which features all his own material with him playing the accordion. Two years later he was back with a second album in November 1989.

By this time, he had already been working on another idea which centred around a Swedish musical based on traditional folk music. In October 1995, *Kristina Från Duvemåla*, the musical he wrote with Björn, premiered in their home country. Based on the novels of Swedish writer Vilhelm Moberg, the show opened to critical acclaim and ran for five years. There is some hope that an English version will make it to

LEFT Benny and his wife, Mona Nörklit

Broadway. Next came Mamma Mia! which involves 24 original ABBA songs. With a play written by the talented Catherine Johnson and the music produced by Björn, with overall production by Judy Craymer, the show was assured of great success. The musical became a huge phenomenon and Benny worked on re-recording the ABBA songs for the movie version of the musical which will hit the big screen in July 2008. Benny still enjoys performing and plays with his own band – the Benny Andersson Orkester, or BAO! for short. The band even plays songs with lyrics written by Björn Ulvaeus from time to time while the 16-piece orchestra supports vocalists Helen Sjöholm and Tommy Körgberg. In April 2007, the band beat a Swedish record when the song "Du Är Min Man" ("You Are My Man") stayed in the charts for 143 weeks.

Songs and performing are not the musician's only forte though. Benny is also a prolific film composer. His first film score came in the early 1970s with *The Seduction Of Inga*. "She's My Kind Of Girl" from the original soundtrack made it to Number 1 in Japan under the title "The Little Girl Of The Cold Wind". But it was to be several years before

Benny once again tackled a film score. The result, in 1987, was *Mio In The Land Of Faraway* where the story is based around the Swedish author Astrid Indgrens Mio. In 2000, he wrote the music for Roy Andersson's Songs From The Second Floor and the music was later re-recorded by BAO! although the songs on the subsequent album contained new lyrics.

After the longest engagement in history, Benny and Frida finally married in 1978, but the engagement was to prove longer than the marriage. The couple were divorced just one year after Björn and Agnetha. Benny then married Mona Nörklit and their son Ludvig was born in 1982.

Following his time with ABBA, Benny won four Swedish Grammys and received the Ivor Novello Award from the British Academy of Composers and Songwriters together with his long-term collaborator Björn. He also won the Music Export Prize from the Swedish Government as well as a Lifetime Achievement Award from the Swedish Music Publishers Association (SMFF). In 2002, Benny Andersson was awarded an honorary professorship by the Swedish Government.

Chapter 4

Björn Ulvaeus

RIGHT Björn to sing, 1975

BJÖRN KRISTIAN ULVAEUS, SOME-times described as the most talented member of ABBA, was born in Gothenburg on 25 April 1945. His family soon moved to Västervik where he went on to study business, economics and law at the University of Lund after completing his military service. But music was his passion and he joined Mackie's Skiffle Group which was formed by two former school mates, Hansi Schwarz and Johan Karlberg. Along with another friend, Tony Rooth, the group performed at parties and schools. They even entered amateur contests before busking across Europe in an old Volvo where they made some money for expenses. By 1962, the group had begun concentrating on folk music and they changed their name to the West Bay Singers. Björn decided to enter

the group in the Plats På Scen an amateur national talent competition. The exposure brought the young band to the attention of Stig Anderson and his partner, record producer Bengt Bernhag who had just formed the Polar Music record label.

West Bay Singers were asked to send in a demo tape to the music company who decided upon hearing the band's numbers to sign them to their label. On the advice of Stig Anderson and Bernhag, the group changed their name to the Hootenanny Singers and entered a talent show singing in Swedish. This was unusual for bands of the time who were used to singing in English. Whether this helped or not, the band won the contest with "Jag Vänter Vid Min Mila". The song was released as a single and became a hit for the

Hootenanny Singers and for the fledgling Polar Music.

In 1964, the band members sat and passed their final school exams which left them free to follow a professional career in music. Their next big hit came with "Gabrielle" later that year and by the end of 1964, the Hootenanny Singers were a major success across Sweden. To coincide with a national folk tour the group released two albums, both of which were called "Hootenanny Singers". The following year saw the band release an album as a tribute to the renowned Swedish songwriter Evert Taube. "Hootenanny Singer Sjunger Evert Taube" did well across their fan base, however, the group were desperate to change their style. Björn, of all the members of the band, was particularly keen to find a way into the more desirable pop scene. The former American hootenanny music that had greatly influenced their music up to this point became less and less important as the group veered towards a more British style, including the Beatles.

For the second album in 1965, Björn wrote two new compositions, "Time To Move Along" and "No Time" while the album "International" also included what was to become a major hit for the band – "Björkens Visa". The years 1964 to 1966 included releasing some singles in the UK, US, France, Belgium, Denmark, Germany, Italy and the Netherlands as well as Norway and Spain. It didn't prove to be a particularly success-ful time. However, they scored a massive hit with "No Time" in South Africa. One of the band's B-sides, "Baby Those Are The Rules", written by Björn was a success on

FAR LEFT Björn and Agnetha skating, 1979

LEFT Star and guitar, 1974

home territory. Moderate success abroad was followed by another album, "Många Ansikten" ("Many Faces"), and the A-side "Marianne" proved to be another hit for the group.

National Service was a pre-requisite for Rooth, Karlberg and Björn. As a German citizen, Schwarz didn't have to do National Service but the other three members of the band all joined the Lifeguards in June 1966. The day before their military service was due to begin, the Hootenanny Singers met the Hep Stars just outside Ålleberg and told the successful contemporary group about a farewell party that evening. Benny and Björn met that night and began their long-term partnership that would see them become producers for Polar Music, members of ABBA and co-writers of three successful musicals. Their partnership is still strong today.

The summer of 1966 saw Benny and Björn compose their first song together, "Isn't It Easy To Say". Unlike the three members of the Hootenanny Singers, the Hep Stars had been granted leave from National Service as their musical contribution to Sweden was considered more important. After finishing his National Service, Björn went to

university and decided to work at Polar Music in his spare time so that he could learn more about the music profession. It was around this time that the group's album "Civilians" was released which contained a number of cover versions of US country and folk songs which was based on the same sort of style as Tom Jones's "Green, Green Grass Of Home". This particular song from the popular stalwart was without a doubt, one of the biggest hits that the Hootenanny Singers would have in January 1967.

Björn's first solo single came in 1968 when he released "Raring". At this point, he seemed to be the only member of the band that thought that a career in pop music was still possible. Another single, "Fröken Fredriksson", became another hit for the newly found soloist. Both the first two singles were covers of US hits, but the B-side of each record were Björn's own compositions. He was still performing – on tour – with the Hootenanny Singers and releasing records, and the group went on to release two further albums in 1968. It was also decided, by the other members of the group, that the Hootenanny Singers would abandon all hope of becoming a pop band. Instead, they focused on producing entirely traditional Swedish numbers which included an album which was written as a tribute to Carl Michael Bellman, the Swedish 18th century composer. The following year saw Björn release two more singles, the second of which was co-written with Benny Andersson and is tongue-in-cheek about the affects of too much partying.

"The Best Of The Hootenanny Singers And Björn Ulvaeus" was released in 1969, but in the spring, Karlberg left the group to work for his father's company when he thought his performing days were over. The group's follow-up album was aptly named "With The Three Of Us". And, even though there were now only three of them, Björn wanted to follow other pursuits as a stand-alone artist while also co-writing material with Benny. However, the differences didn't seem to make much difference to the Hootenanny Singers. They still continued to tour and still released new albums. There were new albums in 1970, 1971 and 1972 but by the following year Björn was busier than ever writing with Benny Andersson, while the two women in their respective lives, Agnetha and Anni-Frid (Frida) were contributing more and more to the two men's backing vocals. On a personal level, Björn and Agnetha had two children, Linda (born 1973) and Christian (born 1977). Another album paying homage to Evert Taube was released by the Hootenanny Singers in 1974 – it was to be the last album that Björn would make with the group. "People Need Love" was the first time that a four-way collaboration between the two couples that formed ABBA took place and it was to mark a turning point.

That same year was to be instrumental in turning ABBA's fortunes around and Björn found himself concentrating on his new group as their faces were splashed across newspapers worldwide when they won the Eurovision Song Contest in April 1974. After his marriage to Agnetha ended in divorce in 1980, Björn married music journalist Lena Kallersjö on 6 January 1981 and the couple had two daughters, Emma (born 1982) and Anna (born 1986). When ABBA split nine years after their historic Eurovision win, Björn and Benny decided to continue their collaboration by co-writing the musical Chess.

Chapter 5

Agnetha Fältskog

IN APRIL 2004, AGNETHA RELEASED a single "If I Thought You'd Ever Change Your Mind" from the album "My Colouring Book", as a comeback after years of living as a recluse since the infamous ABBA split in 1982. The song, originally a hit for Cilla Black in 1969, was released to coincide with the 30th anniversary of victory at the Eurovision Song Contest in 1974. Under the Warner label, the company were confident that Agnetha's comeback would revive her career and stated that "the new CD will be one of our biggest releases this year…It's a big deal for us because she's a megastar – a name that everyone knows". A Warner spokesman went on to state that: "She has such a distinctive voice that you know who is singing immediately."

In 1987, Warner had released Agnetha's solo album "Stand Alone" although the fact that the album didn't do well was blamed on poor publicity through lack of promotion. Rumours that money was behind Agnetha's decision to record again in 2004 were rife when figures suggested in 2002 that she made just £30,000 opposed to the £4 million fortune that she was supposed to have received when the band split more than 20 years earlier. With the release of the new album it looked as if, for a while at least, Agnetha's days as a recluse were over.

She was spotted in a Stockholm club, the Spy Bar, close to the launch date and caused a stir among the other clientele by simply being there. However, the blonde singer had spent two decades living alone on the tiny and remote island of Ekero off the coast of the

RIGHT In full voice on stage

Swedish capital. During her time alone, Agnetha is known to have suffered from a number of phobias including flying, open spaces, crowds and heights, and she underwent treatment to overcome her difficulties. But, despite her desire to remain obsessively private following her fame with ABBA, Agnetha paid to release "My Colouring Book" to relaunch her career.

Known in Sweden as "Garbo II" – for feeling haunted by her overwhelming fame during ABBA's heyday – Agnetha confused and baffled those who didn't understand why someone who was almost destroyed by the fame and hysteria of being in a phenomenal band, should want to make a comeback. But there is possibly a simple explanation. Agnetha could have wanted to regain some control and show that she hadn't just faded away into oblivion. Made up of 1960s cover versions, the new album was nostalgic for the star (and her fans) and marked the period before her rise to fame with ABBA when she had a successful solo career.

Born on 4 May 1950 in Jönköping, Sweden, Agneta (she added the "h" to her name later) Fältskog was the older daughter of Ingvar and Birgit Fältskog.

RIGHT Agnetha on
stage, 1979

Her father was the manager of a department store but had a keen interest in music and show business. Inspired by her father's enthusiasm, Agnetha began a successful career as a solo artist aged just 18. She clocked up a number of chart singles and had some best-selling albums with romantic songs that were "pretty" and catchy which included numbers such as "Som Gladije" – with lyrics by Stig Anderson – "If These Tears Were Gold" and "Mina Ögon".

Her career began when Agnetha was 15 years old and she joined the local dance band as a vocalist. Her songwriting abilities provided her with a Swedish Number 1 with "I Was So In Love" in 1967. She discovered she had a talent for both writing and performing and went on to establish herself as one of the most popular female vocalists in her home country. Agnetha also worked in Germany for a time in 1968 where she released singles in German in collaboration with German legendary songwriter Dieter Zimmermann who was her fiancé for a short time. Seven years later – despite being hugely successful with ABBA – Agnetha continued with her solo career and in 1975 released the

album "Eleven Women In A House" where several songs were described by some critics as having a Kate Bush feel.

A year after she met Björn Ulvaeus, Agnetha became romantically involved with the singer/songwriter when they appeared on a Swedish television programme together in 1969. Following their divorce, the couple continued to work together for a further two years before the group split in 1982. After ABBA decided to "take a break" in the early 1980s, Agnetha went on to release three albums in English. She received moderate success in Europe – mainly in Scandinavia – and in the summer of 1982 she starred in Raskenstam – a Swedish movie for which she won praise for her acting debut.

Her first solo album following ABBA came in 1983. "Wrap Your Arms Around Me" was a moderate hit in the US and Australia and made the charts in Scandinavia selling 1.2 million copies worldwide. It went to Number 1 in both Denmark and Belgium and hit the Number 2 spot in the Netherlands. It received a mixed reaction with *Rolling Stone* magazine claiming that the "treacly...outing doesn't do [Agnetha] justice..." while *Stereo Review* disagreed

RIGHT Happy after winning Eurovision, 1974

and stated that it was "highly entertaining". But mixed reviews shouldn't have worried the star who received a Best Female Artist award back home in Sweden. Two years later, "Eyes Of A Woman" was released but it failed to reach the same heights as her previous album. "I Stand Alone" was released by Warner in 1987 but didn't do as well as expected. Produced by Peter Cetera and Bruce Gaitsch, it became a minor hit in Europe – although in Sweden it spent eight weeks at the top of the charts – and sold 500,000 copies worldwide.

Agnetha disappeared from public view in 1988 to retreat to her remote island and her phobias. It was well known that, of all the members of ABBA, Agnetha was the one who hated the fame and accompanying hysteria that followed the group wherever they went. Despite her musical talents she would have been just as at home, and just as happy, remaining a housewife bringing up her two children, Linda and Christian. Agnetha hated the touring side of the business which was often gruelling, and she was often physically sick before going on stage. Her phobia of crowds came about due to the masses of fans that shouted and became

hysterical. It drove a fear into her and she describes in her autobiography: "There's a very thin line between an ecstatic roar and aggressive screaming. It marks your character and turns into phobias." *As I Am*, her autobiography was published in 1996.

For the sake of ABBA, Agnetha and Björn claimed that their divorce was amicable. As is so often the case, it was anything but. So with a great deal of relief she turned her back on show business when she moved to Ekero, where she craved silence. For 10 years, Agnetha did not play, sing or listen to music. Her time was spent in more holistic pursuits including yoga and alternative medicines. She dated Lars Ericsson (the ice hockey star) before teaming up with the fashion designer Dick Haakonsson. She later had a relationship with ThorBjörn Brander, the detective assigned to her after her children received kidnapping threats, but the relationship didn't last. Then in 1990 she married Tomas Sonnenfeld who was a surgeon. The marriage lasted three years and ended in divorce in 1993.

In 1997 Agnetha met Dutchman Gert van der Graff who was 16 years her junior. Even though Agnetha knew that

RIGHT Agnetha on film, 1982

van der Graff was obsessed with her – and had been for some time – she still allowed herself to begin a relationship with him. In 2000, Agnetha wrote a letter to van der Graff telling him that she wished to be alone and that there was no hope for the two of them. The obsessed Dutchman was charged with threatening behaviour following the letter. The relationship ended in legal action and van der Graff was deported but returned to Sweden a year later. The Swedish police stepped up their surveillance of him when Agnetha returned to the limelight by making a comeback. The relationship had done nothing to enhance Agnetha's image. She was perceived to have become weird by embarking on a relationship with someone who was renowned for being obsessed with her whereas before she took up with van der Graff the Swedish public at large felt sympathy for the former star. In court it emerged that Agnetha admitted to having a relationship with her obsessive fan whereas before she had convincingly denied any involvement with the Dutchman.

After announcing that she was to make a comeback, Agnetha received an ominous letter which was taken seriously by Swedish police as a death threat. Despite her own in-house security team she was assigned a 24-hour guard and bodyguards were flown to her home to protect her.

Although Agnetha cultivated her mysterious image to some extent, it is known that she craves affection and a normal life. Very much her own woman, she still wants to prove that she has got what it takes, but on her own terms. Unfortunately, the publicity that surrounds a megastar making a public return to the limelight is bound to produce a considerable amount of attention. That's the name of the game, but the beautiful and talented Agnetha doesn't like playing by all the rules – and why should she?

Chapter 6

Anni-Frid Lyngstad

ANNI-FRID (FRIDA) SYNNI LYNG-stad was born on 15 November 1945 in Ballangen, near Narvik in Norway. Her mother, Synni Lyngstad had a relationship with a married German sergeant, Alfred Haase, when Germany occupied Norway during the Second World War. It was not an easy beginning for the legendary vocalist whose mother faced a great deal of stigmatism following her liaison. As a result, Frida, and her grandmother, Arntine Lyngstad, were forced to leave their home in 1947. The anger felt by the small Norwegian community towards anyone who had dared to fraternise with Germans during occupation was immense.

Frida's mother was regularly spat upon and abused by her own community for having a German's baby but there wasn't just the danger of reprisals.

There was a real threat that Anni-Frid could be removed from her mother's care – and at the time that would have been a normal consequence to the situation that Anni-Frid's mother faced. Frida eventually settled in a new home in Eskilstuna close to Torshälla on the Swedish side of the border. Her mother remained in Norway where she worked until she became too ill – caused probably by the abuse she suffered from the stigma of having had a German soldier's baby. She died, aged just 21 from kidney disease soon after arriving in Sweden where she was reunited with her daughter and mother. Alfred Haase had promised to return to Norway after the war, but he didn't keep his promise. He later claimed he had not known of Synni Lyngstad's pregnancy.

Raised by her grandmother, Frida

believed her father had died when the naval ship he was on during the war was sunk deliberately. However, she was reunited in 1977 with the man she had never seen, when her biography was published in the German teen magazine *Bravo*. Despite their reunion, today, father and daughter are no longer in contact even though Haase pleaded with Frida to resume contact sometime in 2005 through an article in a German magazine.

Despite the cruel twist of fate that started her life, Frida was destined for great things. Encouraged by her grandmother, Frida first sang in public at the age of 10 for an event arranged by the Red Cross. By the age of 13 she was singing professionally for a local dance band in Eskilstuna. She lied and said she was 16 to get the job and later began a career with Bengt Sardlind's big band where she fell in love with Ragnar Frederiksson. The couple went on to form the Anni-Frid 4 and later married and had two children, Hans and Liselotte.

Not content with her professional life, Frida entered a number of local talent contests – which she won – and she competed in the prestigious SVT's Hyland's Corner. Victory in the competition gave her the opportunity to sign for EMI aged 21 but that signing was a surprise as a result of the contest. This part of the prize for winning the "Nya Ansikten" ("New Faces") contest had been kept from the contestants. Interestingly, Frida's win that night coincided with Sweden's biggest motoring change. The entire country swapped from driving on the left to driving on the right...it was 3 September 1967. However, despite the prestigious win, success eluded her and it wasn't until she met Benny Andersson in 1969 that her fortunes would change. Her first single and those that followed during the next three years were not a commercial success for Frida or her record label, EMI. A couple made it to the lower regions of the radio charts but none did well on the sales chart. However, the press loved Frida and she received a great deal of airplay although it did nothing to make her a household name.

There was a great deal of sophistication in Frida's voice and lack of chart success didn't mean that she wasn't good enough to make it as a solo artist. Her voice was natural and relaxed but perhaps the type of songs she was

LEFT In a cobbled street, 1975

releasing weren't doing her any favours. Whatever it was, the mix wasn't right and Frida lacked the recognition she craved. Things began to change in 1969 when she found herself in joint fourth place at the Swedish finals to represent her adopted home country at the Eurovision Song Contest. Between 1968 and 1970, Frida's musical career was taken up with Swedish folkpark venues (a mixture of indoor and outdoor dancehall venues) as well as cabaret. In the autumn of 1969 her collaboration with Benny Andersson on her seventh single "Peter Pan" was to lead to a long-term relationship both professionally and personally.

Exactly 12 months after "Peter Pan", following three years and eight singles for EMI, Frida and Benny began work on her debut album "Frida". It was to prove a high point in her years with EMI. Her version of the co-written Benny and Björn song "Lycka" with lyrics by Stig Anderson was to prove a highly emotive and personal rendition

LEFT In London, 1976

of what was, in effect, an extremely simple song. She proved she had passion, talent, grit and determination. Her style was unique and soulful.

Benny became Frida's producer, lover and eventually her fiancé when her

ABOVE Thumbs up, 1974

marriage to Frederiksson broke down. She continued her solo career – through the early ABBA years – up until 1975. The solo career she had desperately longed for was revived when ABBA took their extended break in 1982. Phil Collins became her producer and at the end of 1982 she released "Something's Going On". The album reached Number 18 in the UK album charts although the

disappointing time for Frida who decided that – after the album peaked at Number 68 in the UK charts for just one week – she was going to continue her career back in Sweden.

The music industry in Scandinavia and the audiences she recorded for were much more accepting of her individual style than the UK and the rest of Europe had been. Frida enjoyed a successful time where she began to contribute to environmental groups. Then, in a surprise move, Frida announced in 1999 that she would no longer be part of the music industry. She stated that she would not record an album or single or sign a record contract ever again.

Today, Frida still lives in her adopted country, Switzerland. She moved there in the mid 1980s and married her long-time boyfriend, Prince Heinrich Ruzzo Reuss, on 26 August 1992. When she married, Frida received the title Her Serene Highness Princess Anni-Frid Reuss of Plauen. Her husband died in 1999 of lymphoma and it was the second tragedy for Frida in two years. In 1998, her daughter Liselotte died in a fatal car crash in the US. Her time in Switzerland is spent in charity work including drug prevention.

album's title track reached a disappointing Number 44. "Shine" was released two years later – it was to be her second and final English album – but it didn't do as well as the first. It proved to be a

RIGHT Frida singing, 2004

FAR RIGHT Arriving at a party, 2006

In an interview in a Dutch women's magazine, Frida showed her forward thinking, philosophical side when she stated: "I am a strong woman and that is because I was raised like that. But I don't only feel connected with strong women. I especially want to make myself strong for women who aren't. With my music I want to give them strength to let things go. Things that make you unhappy, things that hold up your development and which prevent you from leading your own life. On my CD I sing about the instinct to survive. That instinct is buried in us, it might be deep inside of you. My message is especially aimed at the ones who would like to, but don't dare. I would say, make something of it. You can do it. I'm sure you can."

Stig Anderson

KNOWN FOR HIS STRAIGHT-talking and questioning attitude, Stig Anderson didn't always enjoy an easy relationship with other music bosses and music publishers who felt threatened by him. Anderson was determined that ABBA would win the Eurovision Song Contest and he was also determined that they would break through into the international music scene. One of the most important ideas he had for their success was, that to appeal to a truly European (initially) and then international audience, the songs had to be in English. This would prove difficult for Benny and Björn whose first language was obviously Swedish. However, with Anderson's drive, energy and enthusiasm, the lyrics for "Waterloo" were written and the rest is basically history.

Born Stig Erik Anderson on 25 January 1931 in Hova, Sweden, he grew up in relative poverty with his mother, Ester Anderson. His mother was resourceful and her son inherited her attitude to life. Anderson took on different kinds of jobs at an early age and was greatly influenced by the old gramophone and six 78rpm records that his mother managed to buy when he was around five years old. He enjoyed singing in front of an audience and as a teenager he and his

cheap guitar were frequenting local venues. He found himself rejected by a local girl which led him to writing a ballad. Aged just 16, he wrote "Tivedshambo" ("Hambo From Tived") which was the first of his songs to be recorded later in 1951 – the song was set to become one of his best-known.

During the 1950s he made some headway as a singer/ songwriter but had taken a job as a teacher to maintain some financial stability for his wife and three children.

His first big breakthrough came in 1958 when the Swedish football hero Nacka Skoglund recorded "Vi Hanger Me" ("We're Still Here"). Anderson's song spent 20 weeks in the charts peaking at Number 6. He acquired the nickname "Stikkan" which is what he would be known by in his native Sweden for the remainder of his life – outside Sweden he was always known as Stig.

Then, in late 1959, Lill-Babe sang Anderson's "Are You Still In Love With Me, Klas-Göran" which was recorded by his long-time friend Bengt Bernhag – one of Sweden's top record producers. It was recorded as a comedy number against the writer's wishes, but this turned out to be its biggest asset and it went on to become one of the country's biggest songs in 1960. He established his own publishing company, Sweden Music, where he concentrated on importing songs which he would then translate into Swedish himself. As his empire grew – despite some tough years financially in the early 1960s – Anderson found his niche as a lyricist with cover versions of hits such as "Green, Green Grass Of Home", "You Don't Have To Say You Love Me", "Honey" and "The Most Beautiful Girl", to name a few.

In 1963, Anderson and record producer Bengt Bernhag founded Polar Music. The first signing to the label was the Hootenanny Singers – with of course – Björn Ulvaeus. The band proved popular throughout the 1960s for Polar and when Björn brought in Benny Andersson who was singing with the Hep Stars the songwriting trio of Stig, Björn and Benny was born. The relationships that developed between the three men cultivated a dynamism that brought Stig Anderson his first Swedish Grammy with "Mamma Är Lik Sin Mamma" ("Mum Is Just Like Her Mum").

One of the first works written by the trio was "Ljuva Sextital" ("The Good Old Sixties") which became a major hit, but the death of Bernhag in the early 1970s saw Björn and Benny join Polar

Music as house producers where they all continued developing their songwriting collaboration. He was instrumental in ABBA's approach to the Eurovision Song Contest and, from the winning night, concentrated his efforts on raising their international profile. This saw his own work as a lyricist in decline as he put more and more time into ABBA's songs and their worldwide promotion. While ensuring that ABBA were moving in the right direction on a global scale, back in Sweden Anderson was building his publishing empire with acquisitions of many major Swedish publishing companies. In the late 1980s, he sold Polar Music to PolyGram – which later became part of a merger with Universal Music.

By this time, his relationship had started to take a downturn with ABBA and its former band members. But, it was about to get a whole lot worse for all concerned. Anderson had remained a dominant figure in the band's career and represented their commercial interests and global success through many successful record deals. The mid-1980s revealed that a considerable amount of ABBA's fortune had been lost by mismanagement, unsound investments

and high tax demands which led to a breakdown in relationships with Frida, Agnetha, Benny and Björn. It was claimed that Anderson had been taking a percentage of the profits – of which the band was unaware – for many years. ABBA had also only received

ABOVE Brighton, 1974

royalties of three per cent whereas a contract established much earlier on had cited royalty fees at nine per cent. It is estimated that he profited from around £4.5 million. As a result, members of ABBA submitted a complaint against their former manager with the Stockholm District Court. Agnetha's company, Agnetha Fältskog Produktion AB, Mono Music AB – Benny Andersson's company, the Swiss investors that Frida had sold her investments to and Björn's company all participated in the complaint, but the

lawsuit was eventually settled out of court. Anderson's argument over the lower royalty fee was that a higher fee would only be paid if the group made more records. He claimed it was a pre-requisite. If they didn't make new records, and that had already been confirmed by Björn and Benny as impossible, then the three per cent was final. Anderson was hurt and bitter by the legal action taken against him. He had always tried to have fair business dealings.

Sadly, the legal action meant that Agnetha, Benny and Björn were unable to remain friends with Anderson although Frida, who had sold her shares in Polar Music long before the troubles began was able to remain friends with him. Björn did try to re-establish his relationship with Anderson but the former manager refused to take his calls. He felt that he had done absolutely everything he could have done, and more, to ensure that ABBA were instantly recognisable worldwide. He had ensured they were famous. He had conducted all the deals for them – often this was not easy – and he had invested their money wisely according to his close sources. He felt that he had given

LEFT Frida arrives at the 2004 Polar Music Prize which was founded by Stig Anderson

them everything and had been more than a manager to them; for him, the legal action was a huge breach of loyalty and friendship. He just couldn't forgive.

Anderson established the Polar Music prize which was first awarded in 1992. Major recipients of the award include Bob Dylan, Sir Paul McCartney, Joni Mitchell, Stevie Wonder and Bruce Springsteen. He generally retired during the mid-1990s although, despite having sold Polar Music, he continued to remain active within the company. Stig Anderson had a heart attack on 12 September 1997 and died at the age of 66. Even 10 years after his death, his influence is still evident in the Swedish music industry. The Stikkan Anderson double CD is a celebration of his lyrics and music. The Swedish music entrepreneur is celebrated by a memorial which sits proudly in the square in his home town of Hova. The bronze bust of Stikkan Anderson was made by local artist Jessica Lindholm.

Chapter 8

The ABBA Name

THE ACRONYM ABBA COMES FROM the four members of the band's first initials: Agnetha, Björn, Benny and Anni-Frid. At first there was some confusion over whether the group could use the name ABBA as it was also the name of a Swedish canned fish company. However, with his usual panache, Stig Anderson concluded a deal with the company and ABBA was born.

Originally, the band had used the name Festfolk, which also meant "engaged couples" and "party people" before working under their own first names. Festfolk didn't work for the band and they didn't achieve much success under this name. Equally, using Björn & Benny, Agnetha & Anni-Frid was rather long-winded and it was decided – after some consultation and smooth operating by Anderson that ABBA was a much more viable option.

BELOW ABBA stage backdrop, 1975

Chapter 9

The Music – Albums and Singles

THE TWO KEY INGREDIENTS IN the music of ABBA were the vocals of Agnetha (soprano) and Frida (mezzo-soprano) mixed with the keyboard style that was very much Benny's own. Each song consisted of a strong melody that was interspersed with moments of experimentation often provided by sound engineer Michael Tretow. The early 1970s saw the group try a number of styles but by 1975 they had established a multi-layer effect with pleasing harmonies. In the early 1980s ABBA returned to the more basic productions that had dominated their music a decade earlier – with synthesizers playing a vital role in their unique style of pop.

The Albums

"Ring Ring"

When the first album was released in Sweden on 26 March 1973, the group weren't even called ABBA. Only after the title track became a hit did the four musicians decide to make their collaboration more permanent.

Highest chart position: Number 2 Sweden and Norway

"Waterloo"

First released on 4 March 1974, "Waterloo" began in the recording studio in September 1973. The album was already well under way before ABBA

submitted their entry to the Eurovision Song Contest in 1974. It was the first album released under the name ABBA.
Highest chart position: Number 1 Sweden and Norway

"ABBA"

Following on from Eurovision success, recording sessions began in August 1974 for the third album "ABBA" which was released in April 1975. The multi-layered sound for which the group became synonymous was firmly established with this album.
Highest chart position: Number 1 Sweden, Norway, Australia and Zimbabwe

"Greatest Hits"

On 17 November 1975, ABBA released their "Greatest Hits" album which was their first compilation. The song "Fernando" was only included on the album for certain releases during the first few months of 1976.
Highest chart position: Number 1 Sweden, Norway, UK and Zimbabwe

"Arrival"

This was first released on 11 October 1976 following lengthy recording sessions between August 1975 and September 1976. It was to spawn some of the group's greatest hits including "Dancing Queen" and "Money, Money,

Money ". It was also the album that pushed their direct pop style to the limit.

Highest chart position: Number 1 Australia, Belgium, Mexico, New Zealand, Norway, Sweden, the Netherlands, UK, West Germany and Zimbabwe

"ABBA – The Album"
Released on 12 December 1977, this album included a number of longer tracks with more complex musical structures than fans were used to. The album was released to coincide with *ABBA – The Movie* which premiered in cinemas worldwide.

Highest chart position: Number 1 Belgium, Mexico, New Zealand, Norway, Sweden, Switzerland, the Netherlands and the UK

"Voulez-Vous"
Recording began on "Voulez-Vous" in March 1978 and continued for 12 months before it was finally released on 23 April 1979. This sixth album was recorded at a time when the entire world was in the grip of "disco fever".

Highest chart position: Number 1 Argentina, Belgium, Finland, Japan, Mexico, Norway, Sweden, Switzerland, UK, West Germany and Zimbabwe

"Greatest Hits Vol 2"

The second compilation album for the group was released on 29 October 1979. It was essentially a round-up of all the hits since the first compilation record and was released to coincide with ABBA's tour of Europe and the US.

Highest chart position: Number 1 Belgium, Canada and the UK

"Gracias Por La Música"

The album was first released in Sweden on 23 June 1980 and was titled and recorded in Spanish to help the group break through into the South American market. The Spanish version of "Dancing Queen" was entitled "Reina Danzante" for the album, but renamed "Reina Del Baile" before its release.

Highest chart position: Number 4 Argentina

"Super Trouper"

Released on 3 November 1980, "Super Trouper" was recorded between February and October 1980. The divorce between Björn and Agnetha just prior to the album's release was highlighted in the track "The Winner Takes It All".

Highest chart position: Number 1

Belgium, Mexico, Norway, Sweden, Switzerland, the Netherlands, UK, West Germany and Zimbabwe

"The Visitors"

Recordings for the group's eighth album took place between March 1981 and November of that year. It was released on 30 November 1981 and was described by critics as "bleak". However, it won critical acclaim with fans.

Highest chart position: Number 1 Belgium, Norway, Sweden, Switzerland, the Netherlands, UK, West Germany and Zimbabwe

"The Singles – The First Ten Years"
The album was released on 8 November 1982 and marked the end of ABBA's career as a group. Originally, the group had planned to record new songs – just as they had done every year – but all four members felt that their energy had gone and produced this double album instead.
Highest chart position: Number 1 Belgium, South Africa and the UK

"ABBA Live"
ABBA fans had demanded a live album for many years. The group had traditionally always been against the idea but this album finally gave the fans what

they wanted, four years after the group had split. It was released in August 1986 with most of the tracks coming from ABBA's concert at Wembley in 1979, while others came from the Australian tour two years earlier.

"ABBA Gold"
The album was first released on 21 September 1992 and sold more than 2.2 million copies worldwide. It went on to become one of ABBA's greatest successes with its 19 tracks. It was re-released in 1999 to mark the 25th anniversary of ABBA's success at the Eurovision Song Contest in 1974. It was again released in 2002 to mark the album's 10th anniversary.
Highest chart position: Number 1 Australia, Belgium, France, Germany, Mexico, Norway, Spain, Sweden, Switzerland and the UK

"More ABBA Gold"
The album "More ABBA Gold" was released on 1 June 1993 in Sweden after the original "ABBA Gold" released the previous year had stormed up the charts. A surprise inclusion was the previously unreleased song "I Am The City" which was recorded in one of the

group's final recording sessions in 1982.
Highest chart position: Number 2
Zimbabwe

"Thank You For the Music"
Twelve years after ABBA split up, this
album "Thank You For the Music" was
released on 31 October 1994. This is a
four-CD collection which features
hits, much loved numbers and
previously unreleased songs which
include an alternative version of
"Thank You For The Music", "Dream
World" and a 23-minute medley of
other songs never heard before,
entitled "ABBA Undeleted".

"ABBA Oro"
The album was originally released in
1993 which includes a collection of
songs in Spanish. Then in 1999, the
album was re-released with 15 tracks
collected onto one CD. It was released
again in 2002.
Highest chart position: Number 8
Mexico

"The Definitive Collection"
Released on the 2 November 2001, "The
Definitive Collection" is based on the
same concept as "The Singles – The

First Ten Years". It includes every track that was recorded and released by Polar Music between 1972 and 1982. There are 37 tracks on the album with some songs that were not chosen as Polar A-sides at the time of recording. The album also includes a remix of "Ring Ring" and an extended US remix of "Voulez-Vous".

Highest chart position: Number 3 Korea

The Singles

The singles are too numerous to mention in this book, so the following entries are a list of those numbers that made it into the UK charts only.

"Waterloo"
Released on 20 April 1974, "Waterloo" was the winning entry for the Eurovision Song Contest earlier that same month, made it to the Number 1 spot.

"Ring Ring"
"Ring Ring" had received some moderate success in Sweden before it was released in the UK. It made

the Top 40 in the UK charts, peaking at Number 32.

"I Do I Do I Do I Do I Do"

Released on 12 July 1975, this firm favourite didn't fare as well as its predecessors. It peaked in the charts at Number 38.

"SOS"

This was more like it! "SOS" – released on 20 September 1975 – climbed into the Top 10 reaching Number 6.

"Mamma Mia"

Released on 13 December 1975, "Mamma Mia" gave ABBA their second Number 1 in the UK.

"Fernando"

"Fernando" was also to prove a bit hit for the group. It reached the Number 1 spot in the charts following its release on 27 March 1976. It was to remain chart-bound for a total of 15 weeks.

"Dancing Queen"

Likewise, "Dancing Queen" followed suit and reached Number 1, remaining in the UK charts for 15 weeks. It was released on 21 August 1976. The song was then re-released on 5 September 1992. It peaked at Number 16 and remained in the charts for a total of five weeks.

"Money, Money, Money"

Peaking at Number 3, "Money, Money, Money " stayed in the charts for 12 weeks following its release on 20 November 1976.

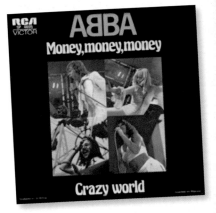

"Knowing Me, Knowing You"

Released on 26 February 1976, this track gave ABBA their fifth Number 1 in the UK charts. It remained in the charts for 13 weeks.

"The Name Of The Game"

Proving that ABBA could be taken seriously, this sixth Number 1 for the group stayed in the charts for 12 weeks. The song was released on 22 October 1977.

"Summer Night City"

"Summer Night City" was smouldering, but it didn't reach the Top 3 in the charts. It peaked at Number 5 and stayed in the charts for just nine weeks. The track was released on 16 September 1978.

"Chiquitita"

This soulful ballad was released on 3 February 1979 and peaked in the charts at Number 2, narrowly missing the hot spot. It remained in the charts for nine weeks.

"Does Your Mother Know"

This track was released on 5 May 1979 and made it to Number 4. It stayed in the UK charts for nine weeks.

"Angeleyes"/"Voulez-Vous"

This double A-side made it to Number 3 in the UK and stayed in the charts for 11 weeks. It was released on 14 July 1979.

"Take A Chance On Me"

Released on 4 February 1978, "Take A Chance On Me" gave the group a seventh Number 1 in the UK charts. It was also the second time that they had had a three successive Number 1 hits. It remained in the charts for 10 weeks.

"Gimme Gimme Gimme (A Man After Midnight)"

Reaching Number 3 and remaining in the UK charts for 12 weeks, this song was released on 20 October 1979.

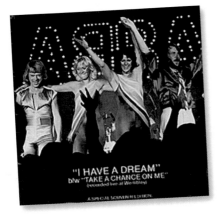

"I Have A Dream"

The smooth, soulful "I Have A Dream" just missed the hot spot when it peaked at Number 2 following its release on 15 December 1979. It stayed in the UK charts for 10 weeks.

"The Winner Takes It All"

With some reference to Björn and Agnetha's recent divorce, this track took ABBA back to the Number 1 slot for their third round of successive chart-topping singles. The song remained in the charts for 10 weeks following its release on 2 August 1980.

"Super Trouper"

This title track from the album of the same name was also to provide the band with a Number 1 – it was their ninth time at the top of the UK charts. Released on 15 November 1980, the track stayed in the charts for 12 weeks.

"Lay All Your Love On Me"

Released on 18 July 1981, "Lay All Your Love On Me" reached Number 7 in the

UK charts. It remained in the charts for seven weeks.

"One Of Us"

On 12 December 1981, the fact that the two couples' relationships were breaking down or had broken down was epitomised in this sad single when it was released. It peaked at Number 3 and remained in the charts for 10 weeks.

"Head Over Heels"

Released on 20 February 1982, "Head Over Heels" reached Number 25 in the UK charts. It stayed chart-bound for just seven weeks.

"The Day Before You Came"

Disappointingly, this track only made it to Number 32 in the UK charts where it stayed for six weeks. It was released on 23 October 1982.

"Under Attack"

"Under Attack" fared slightly better than its predecessor when it made it to Number 26. It was released on 11 December 1982 and remained in the charts for eight weeks.

"Thank You For The Music"

The rousing "Thank You For The Music" peaked in the UK charts at Number 33. Following its release on 12 November 1983 it stayed in the charts for only six weeks.

Other songs that fans will be familiar

with include B-side recordings and some A-sides that didn't make it into the charts, such as:

"People Need Love" (1971) – the first song that features lead vocals with Agnetha and Frida

"Merry-Go-Round" (1972)

"He Is Your Brother" 1972)
"Santa Rosa" (1972)
"Love Isn't Easy" (1973)
"I Am Just A Girl" (1973)
"Honey Honey" (1974)
"King Kong Song" (1974)
"So Long" (1974)
"I've Been Waiting For You" (1974)
"Man In The Middle" (1975)
"Intermezzo No 1" (1975)
"Hey, Hey, Helen" (1976) and
"That's Me" (1976).

The group also found fame with the likes of:
"Crazy World" (1976)
"Happy Hawaii" (1977)
"Wonder" (1977)
"I'm A Marionette" (1977)
"Eagle" (1977)
"Lovelight" (1979)
"Kisses of Fire" (1979)
"The King Has Lost His Crown" (1979)
"Elaine" (1980)
"The Piper" (1980)
"On And On And On" (1981)
"Should I laugh Or Cry" (1981)
"The Visitors" (1982)
"Cassandra" (1982)
"You Owe Me One" (1982) and
"Happy New Year" (1992)

Chapter 10

The Money

STIG ANDERSON WAS AN ASTUTE man and – whether it was shrewdness, a fluke or he meticulously planned the whole thing – he guided the four members of ABBA to fame and fortune with a single-minded devotion. Even those who were enthusiastic in Sweden didn't think that once ABBA had won Eurovision that they could possibly go on to receive the worldwide adoration – and the fortunes that went with it – after the elation of the contest had died down. But they were wrong – very wrong. Stig Anderson reportedly put £20 on ABBA to win – he collected his £400 winnings on 7 April 1974. For him, ABBA winning the Eurovision wasn't the pinnacle of their careers – it was the beginning. He had an extraordinary business acumen that saw him jetting off all over Europe to make

deals for the release of ABBA records. His quest to sign up the group with everyone he could was unusual. Normally, a group would make a deal with one major UK or US company, but that wasn't going to be enough for this curious businessman. He meticulously laid solid foundations between 1974 and 1975 that would make ABBA famous – and rich.

The philosophy wasn't simple and it certainly involved hard work – and tireless travelling and meetings – but it paid off. Rather than giving one major company the rights to ABBA he used Polar Music to directly license the group to as many different countries as he possibly could. This meant a much greater financial gain from each deal and more commitment from the individual countries to sell ABBA records. It was to ultimately make them all millions.

But, Stig Anderson was a canny businessman and even when ABBA became Sweden's largest export behind Volvo he kept a tight rein on the finances and Polar Music continued to employ a moderate 50 staff or so. But, the cost of living and being taxed in Sweden were exceptionally high – even in the 1970s and 1980s. It has the highest tax rate in the world. Even though each of the group was making a huge amount of money, much of it was disappearing in taxes. They were paying a whacking 85% in tax.

LEFT Spinning the wheel, 1978

RIGHT On stage in Denmark

The next idea was for the money to be invested to alleviate some of the tax. It was used in business ventures to spread the risks. The company floated on the stock exchange and each member of the group was liable for 33% capital gains on share sales rather than paying the 85% tax as a private individual. They set up the property company Badhus which was to remain relatively successful. Then came Eastern Europe.

In lieu of cash, Anderson became involved in some strange commodities that ranged from art treasures, rare coins, sports equipment and shirts to Polish potatoes. He believed that he was doing the right thing and that getting in behind the Iron Curtain was the way forward. In a misguided deal, some Iron Curtain record sales were partly paid for with Romanian oil which was imported through a Swedish company which was sold on the Rotterdam spot market. The spot market collapsed and the value of ABBA oil drained away dramatically.

They set up Pol Oil which was to become the biggest mistake of their professional careers. It cost ABBA and Polar Music a fortune and caused a great deal of embarrassment and ultimately a huge falling out which

THE MONEY

would see three members of the band lose their friendships with Stig Anderson for good. Only Frida would remain in touch with their former manager.

With the collapse of the spot market in 1982, it was estimated that the company had spent $39 million buying up company shareholdings and by the end of the year equity accounted for only two per cent on the balance sheet. ABBA were in deep trouble. They had borrowed heavily because of spending money they didn't have and were near to financial collapse. Their subsequent company, Kuban, had its share dealings suspended by the Stockholm Stock Exchange and the band had one option; to sell up.

In another set back, the Swedish revenue discovered that three of the band members – Benny, Björn and Agnetha – had evaded tax payments of around £4.6 million relating to their business affairs. Frida had already sold her shares and was largely unaffected by the action. What that left each member of the band with financially is not clear. What is clear is that it was an ugly end to what had begun for ABBA as an exciting fairytale – all in the pursuit of paying less tax.

Chapter 11

The Music Lives On – ABBA Revival

MORE THAN TWO DECADES HAVE passed since ABBA's "temporary break", when Benny and Björn decided to work on the musical, Chess, and Agnetha and Frida decided to work on their solo careers, and there is still no sign of a grand reunion between the former band members.

However, despite the lack of ABBA, the music has lived on in the form of the musical *Mamma Mia!*, the forthcoming motion picture of the same name and the likes of tribute bands such as Björn Again. Not only that, the 1990s saw the beginning of a major revival in the music of ABBA with a number of hit films using the group's music on their soundtracks

including *Muriel's Wedding*.

In addition, the compilation CD "ABBA Gold" that was released in 1992 has sold more than 26 million copies. The follow-up CD released a year later sold more than two and a half million copies worldwide. The compilation CDs were followed in 1994 by the boxed four CD set of "Thank You For The Music" which included the greatest hits as well as a number of rare and previously unreleased recordings.

When the hugely successful *Mamma Mia!* celebrated its fifth anniversary in April 2004 in London's West End, the performance was attended by Frida, Benny and Björn. In Sweden, the premiere for the musical (which opened

in February 2004) was attended by all four members of the group. It was a momentous occasion for all concerned.

Universal Music, who eventually bought out Polygram (the owner of the original Polar Music), have strived throughout the beginning of the 21st century to keep the ABBA story alive. The multinational giant has continually upgraded the ABBA catalogue and the eight original studio albums: "Ring Ring", "Waterloo", "ABBA", "Arrival", "ABBA – The Album", "Voulez-Vous", "Super Trouper" and "The Visitors" have all been reissued. Each original album's re-release includes additional bonus tracks that are packaged in revised artwork which is accompanied by a comprehensive booklet. In 2004, Universal Music released a new "Waterloo" that came with a DVD of previously unreleased television performances to make the 30th anniversary of the album.

The company have also reissued the compilation albums "ABBA Gold" and "ABBA Oro" – intended for the South American market – with revised booklets and updated notes. There is also a double CD which is compiled of all ABBA's singles. To date, "The Definitive Collection" has sold more than one million copies worldwide. In 2005, Universal released a comprehensive box set entitled "The Complete Studio Recordings" which received rave reviews from critics and fans alike.

There are now two different DVDs of

ABBA's videos which include *The Definitive Collection* and *ABBA Gold*. Both DVDs include re-mastered original film clips. In addition, the two live concert films, *ABBA – The Movie* and *ABBA in Concert*, have both been cleaned up, restored and re-released on DVD with extra material that was previously unseen. Universal Music has also released *Super Trouper – the official documentary –* and *The Last Video* which is a short film which features all four members of the group making cameo appearances.

LEFT In harmony on stage

Chapter 12

Björn Again
– a Tribute

IN 1988, MELBOURNE, AUSTRALIA was the setting for an unlikely concept: an ABBA tribute band. Yet, the idea worked and now almost 20 years later the band Björn Again are still going strong and are as popular as ever. The idea was the brainchild of Rod Leissle and John Tyrrell who both decided that a career change was in order. Renaming themselves, Benny Anderwear and Björn Volvo-us, together with two female band members, known as Agnetha Falstart and Frida Longstokin (all puns on the original band members' names) they formed Björn Again and made their debut at The Tote in Melbourne in 1989. The crowd went wild for this tribute band who not only looked like ABBA, but also sounded like them.

In May 2007, Björn Again played once again at The Tote to celebrate their 18th anniversary as a touring band. Today there are five Björn Again tribute bands which perform throughout the world. To date these tribute bands have played in more than 70 countries. They are managed

by Rod Leissle and his management company with offices in Australia, the UK and North America.

Within two years of forming, Björn Again went on tour and played in Gothenburg where they received a telegram from Björn Ulvaeus which read: "The best of luck. Anyone who looks like me ought to have a successful career!" Although the man himself was impressed with the stage show that Björn Again were putting on, he was not as enamoured with their "Swedish" accents when on Belfast Radio in 1992

he stated: "I am flattered by everything except Björn Again's accents. I hope my accent isn't as lousy!" This was praise – even if he didn't like the accents – and it was incredible that the concept of taking off a band from the past would literally hit the big time.

What a 29-year-old man was doing rooting around in his wardrobe where he found flared trousers and platform shoes is anybody's guess, but Rod Leissle decided – upon finding his old clothes – to listen to 1970s music. He listened to ABBA and was suddenly struck with the idea of putting on a stage show which would revisit the era with its catchy music and outrageous fashion. His belief was that the Swedish band: "globally encapsulated all that was good" and that ABBA were the ideal 1970s phenomenon on which to base his slightly crazy idea.

But his idea was to prove almost a phenomenon itself. Even 33 years after ABBA first came to international attention, Björn Again are still thriving as the tribute band that followed in the footsteps of the original group who took the world by storm. The 1980s with its various new musical genres left ABBA, as a pure pop group, struggling against the competition. By 1987 they were generally considered to have passed their prime. That, combined with tensions within the group and the breakdown of both marriages left ABBA with few places to go professionally. But within two years they would be back – not literally, but their tribute band would spend the months between 1988 and 1989 searching for theatrical ideas to make a stage show exciting while rehearsing music and auditioning singers for Agnetha's and Frida's roles. It quite simply caused a major revolution in the music industry and there was widespread revival and nostalgia.

Following some sell-out concerts in

LEFT London – Family Prom in the Park

RIGHT Björn Again –
Australia

Melbourne, Björn Again toured Australia where they were featured on several national television shows. Björn Again were quickly establishing themselves as a cult band and in 1990 continued an extensive tour which led to them becoming household names in every state across the country. Having gained a wide following in their home country, the tribute band set off for Sweden, while 1991 saw them maintaining a hectic touring schedule. It was around this time that Björn Again employed Paul Franklin as their agent.

"ABBA Gold" was released on CD – the first time the band had been released on the latest technology – in 1992 and in the run up to its release, Björn Again were invited to perform on national television in Sweden. The reception they received was tremendous and they undertook an intense tour of Europe (including Scandinavia). The tour took in *The Jonathan Ross Show* and the Reading Festival and seven consecutive sell-out shows at the Town and Country Club (now the Forum) in London. They went on to perform "Dancing Queen" with U2 in Stockholm. The same year, Benny and Björn invited Björn Again to meet with them on their visit to

Stockholm. The band then found huge critical acclaim on the UK's University circuit and had their first gig at the Royal Albert Hall where the concert was, once again, a sell-out.

In 1994, the huge Australian hit movie, *Muriel's Wedding*, included a number of ABBA songs and director PJ Hogan invited Björn Again to perform live at the Cannes Film Festival. The band then played at London's Gay Pride to an audience of more than 300,000 before embarking on their first North American tour. It was not long before the tribute band had played their 1,000th concert and the following year saw them touring back in Australia, North America, the UK and Europe.

In 1996, the band began a gruelling tour around the UK before starting their world tour which also saw them performing in Hong Kong, Japan and Ireland. The trip to Hong Kong was particularly memorable for the band as they were invited to play at the Royal Hong Kong Yacht Club as part of the official celebrations when Hong Kong was handed back to China.

To mark their 10th anniversary in 1998, Björn Again were back at the Royal Albert Hall for a sell-out show

before making an appearance at the Gay Games in Amsterdam. They were the support act for the Spice Girls on two occasions before they began yet another UK tour. The following year saw them open at the Glastonbury Festival where they were a huge success. Next came a "fly on the wall" documentary by Channel 5 which went on to win a coveted Rose D'or award. They then celebrated 150 years of Harrods with owner Mohammed Al Fayed. Björn Again saw in the new millennium with three parties including a private function with Rowan Atkinson, a street party in Belfast and a show in Newcastle. It was also the year (1999) that *Mamma Mia!* was to open in London's West End.

Fans of Björn Again demanded more tours and the New Year was to see the band set off on tours in the UK, the rest of Europe, North America (there were three tours running simultaneously). The band also performed at the launch of CCTV, the Chinese television channel where it was estimated that they were watched by one billion people worldwide. The following three years were just as busy for the band with appearances at Hyde Park with Shania

LEFT London – Family Prom in the Park

Twain and a concert to mark the New Year at the Millennium Dome. They would support the American singer a year later on her own tour.

The loss of Malcolm Kingsnorth the band's tour manager and sound engineer – in 2004 was devastating for the band and they held a Benefit Concert in his honour along with Billy Connolly and other household names. Björn Again also went on tour with Cher in 2004 and played at Russell Crowe's wedding. The next year saw Björn Again as busy as ever, but highlights from 2006 include being invited by Jasper Carrott to perform at his Rock With Laughter as well as performing at JK Rowling's Masquerade Ball in aid of Scotland's MS Society.

From a crazy idea to a world renowned band, Björn Again is as popular as ever and there's no sign that the music of ABBA will lose its appeal with worldwide audiences anytime soon.

LEFT Music Midtown Festival, Atlanta, Georgia

Chapter 13

Mamma Mia!
– The Stage Show

WITH SHOWS IN LONDON, NEW York's Broadway, Las Vegas, Japan, Moscow, Hamburg, Stuttgart, Gothenburg and Madrid, along with North American and international tours, the stage show *Mamma Mia!* named after ABBA's chart-topper of 1975, is one of the most popular stage shows ever. In fact, it is so popular and has been seen by so many audiences throughout the world that it has become a global musical phenomenon – just like the band's music on which the show is based.

Playwright Catherine Johnson teamed up with Benny and Björn to create something unusual and unique in *Mamma Mia!* Johnson's story evolves around a young girl named Sophie who lives on a fictional Greek island with her mother Donna. Sophie is about to marry her fiancé Sky, but is marred by the knowledge that she doesn't know her father. Donna, who runs the local taverna, is reluctant to talk to her daughter about the past. Undeterred by her mother's unwillingness to divulge who her father is, Sophie discovers an old diary which describes three dates her mother went on with three different men. Without her mother's knowledge, or approval, the young girl invites all three men to her forthcoming wedding.

All three men arrive. Harry Bright is a banker with an interesting laugh, while Bill Austin is typically Australian. Sam

Carmichael had an affair with Donna 20 years previously, despite being engaged to someone else. For her part, Donna invites two old friends (Rosie and Tanya), who used to sing with her in Donna and the Dynamos, to come to her daughter's wedding.

Donna has already told Sophie that the taverna was built with money that came from an inheritance. Sophie is also told that she is named after the benefactor, Sophia, who is Bill Austin's aunt. It is natural for Sophie to assume that he is her father and she asks him to give her away. However, after some confusion and mix-ups, the other two potential fathers believe that they will be giving their "daughter" away. Meanwhile, Sophie writes them all notes to say that Donna will give her away, however, she and Sky are wondering whether they know each other well enough to marry after all. Sam and Donna have a bitter row over Sophie's parentage where it becomes apparent to them both that they are still deeply in love. The wedding day arrives – and bride and groom decide to proceed with the nuptials – where it is made obvious that Sophie's paternity cannot be proved. All decide that it doesn't matter and all three

men wish to remain a part of her life.

Sophie and Sky then announce to their wedding guests that for the time being they have decided not to marry. Donna and Sam decide to wed instead while Rosie and Bill become mutually attracted. Harry is happy to divulge that he is gay and in a relationship with a man called Laurence – known as Nigel in some productions – while Sophie and Sky decide to travel the world.

Throughout the entire production audience participation is a pre-requisite and with the inclusion of "Dancing Queen", "The Winner Takes It All", "SOS", "Knowing Me, Knowing You", "Take A Chance On Me", "I Do, I Do, I Do, I Do, I Do", "The Name Of The Game", "Money, Money, Money", "Super Trouper", "Gimme! Gimme! Gimme!" and "Mamma Mia!" who could fail to join in? The other ABBA songs included in the musical are; "Honey, Honey", "Thank You For The Music", "Chiquitita", "Lay All Your Love On Me", "Does Your Mother Know", "I Have A Dream", "Voulez-Vous" and, of course, "Waterloo". At the end of 2006, it was estimated that the hit show had been watched by more than 30 million people worldwide.

LEFT A fifth anniversary show in London, 2004

The first *Mamma Mia!* premiered in London at the Prince Edward Theatre on a familiar date (6 April) 1999 while on Broadway, the show took to the stage on 18 October 2001 at the Winter Garden Theatre. In Canada, *Mamma Mia!* was launched at the Royal Alexandra Theatre in Toronto on 23 May 2000. In London, the show transferred to the Prince of Wales Theatre in 2004. With 1,500 performances on 15 May 2005, the musical beat records set by *The Sound Of Music* and *The King And I* and by September 2006 had become the longest running musical on Broadway. It had already become the longest running musical in Las Vegas – a record which it set with its 1,000th performance in June 2005.

So who are the cast and crew behind these incredible shows being performed around the globe? For Benny and Björn a meeting with Sir Tim Rice planted the seeds for writing a musical. While still members of ABBA, the talented duo co-wrote *Chess* with Sir Tim which opened in London's West End in 1986. A year earlier, Benny and Björn had seen their first musical, *Kristina Från Duvemåla*, open in Sweden. The show ran for three years and then in 2002, *Chess* began its own run in Stockholm.

Award-winning Catherine Johnson, who already had a string of plays to her name, wrote the entertaining and "feel-good" story which is interspersed with the musical genius of Benny and Björn. Johnson, who is responsible for successful plays including *Rag Doll*, *Renegades*, *Shang-a-Lang*, *Little Baby Nothing* and *Too Much Too Young*, has won a number of awards for her inspiring work including the Thames Television's Writer-In-Residence Award and Thames Television's Best Play Award. In 2002, Johnson was nominated for a Tony Award for her book *Mamma Mia!*

The concept for using ABBA's music, but in an original musical, was the brainchild of pioneering producer Judy Craymer. She began her career in the theatre with the Haymarket Theatre in Leicester before working on the original production of *Cats* with Cameron Mackintosh in 1981. The following year, Craymer joined Sir Tim Rice's production company, Heartaches, before she became managing director of Three Knights in 1984. Her career

then took her into film and television – including *White Mischief* and *Madame Souzatzka* before Craymer teamed up with Benny and Björn to form Littlestar Services in 1996 along with Richard East. The idea? To produce the stage show *Mamma Mia!*

This was the second time that Craymer had worked with Benny and Björn and she went on to become executive producer of *The Winner Takes It All*, an official documentary about ABBA. Craymer is also executive producer of *Super Troupers: A Celebratory Film From "Waterloo" To "Mamma Mia!"* as well as being the global producer for the hit musical. Judy Craymer's inspirational work with *Mamma Mia!* won her the Woman of the Year Award in 2002. Craymer works closely with Richard East who has been involved in *Mamma Mia!* since the beginning, while Phyllida Lloyd is the show's director. Lloyd has directed opera, theatre and a television film. The film of *Mamma Mia!* will be this dynamic director's first major movie.

No musical is complete without a choreographer and *Mamma Mia!* is no exception with Anthony van Laast taking charge of the role. He was

LEFT *Mamma Mia!* in New York

awarded the MBE for his services to dance and choreography in 1999. Other members of the crew include the production designer, Mark Thompson, who regularly works with the Royal Shakespeare Company (RSC) and Howard Harrison, who is in charge of lighting design and who also won the Australian Green Room Award for his work on *Mamma Mia!* The sound designers are Bobby Aitken, who has more than 20 years experience and Andrew Bruce. Martin Koch is the talented musician in charge of musical supervision.

RIGHT Sir Cameron Mackintosh attends the Royal Charity Gala Performance of the musical *Mamma Mia!*, 2004

In London, the cast is headed up by Hannah Robertson who plays Sophie, Linzi Hateley (Donna), Paul Shelford (Sky), Steven Finch (Harry Bright), Paul Hawkyard (Bill Austin), Iain Fletcher (Sam Carmichael) with Joanna Monro (Rosie) and Jane Gurnett who plays Tanya. Reviews have included: "Fresh and exhilarating" from the *Sunday Express* while the *Daily Mail* describes it as "Sheer enjoyability – a five star performance". Charles Spencer of the *Daily Telegraph* wrote "The perfect ticket for a feel-good night out" while *The Guardian* described the experience as "…great fun".

MAMMA MIA! – THE STAGE SHOW

line. While being swept along by the ingenious choreography and witty dialogue, I found myself examining ABBA's music in a new light."

Having had audiences of more than one million, the hit show in Las Vegas celebrated four successful years in February 2007 while the North American tour set a box office record in Arkansas at the Walton Arts Centre where it grossed more than $543,950 for eight sell-out performances between 13-18 February 2007. Equally, although the show was due to close in Madrid in June 2007, more than one million people had flocked to see the musical in its 1,000 performances. On 6 April 2007, *Mamma Mia!* in London celebrated its eighth birthday while earlier that month, the show was well received by audiences in Dubai.

The International Tour then went on to Riga in Latvia. The International Tour has also visited South Africa, Estonia, Portugal, Belgium, France,

Reviews from the other side of the Atlantic are equally rapturous with Matt Wolf of Associated Press announcing that it is "Quite simply a phenomenon!" His praise is echoed by *The Today Show* in Australia which says its "The best night out you'll ever have". The highest praise so far has come from David Sinclair at *The Times* who said: "A production of tremendous warmth, vitality and technical excellence that offers an evening of unbridled fun. It is a tribute to the scriptwriting skill of Catherine Johnson that the ABBA songs are slotted so naturally into the story-

RIGHT Frida Lyngstad attends the Royal Charity Gala Performance of the musical *Mamma Mia!* with producer, Judy Craymer

Germany, Austria and Switzerland. In the summer of 2007, the tour played in Shanghai, China for four weeks. In March 2007, the Moscow production celebrated its 200th show which has been seen by 250,000 since it opened in October 2006. September 2006 saw the final show in Hamburg and in Ireland the show enjoyed six weeks at the Point Theatre in Dublin for the second time.

Founded in 1993 by Evelyn H Lauder, of Estée Lauder, the Breast Cancer Research Foundation (BCRF) is a non-profit organisation that is dedicated to funding clinical and genetic research. The charity is supported by *Mamma Mia!* after Judy Craymer and Evelyn Lauder got talking on a transatlantic flight which resulted in a pink and white Rock Chick Supremo T-shirt. The T-shirt is sold today at shows in London, Broadway, Las Vegas and on tour as well as being available on-line. This fund raising campaign has seen more than £240,000 going to breast cancer charities worldwide. All scientists who work with the BCRF are cutting edge innovators who are dedicated to finding an established cure that will wipe out this cancer. The BCRF is an innovative and prolific organisa-

tion that was named by *Money Magazine* as one of the top eight charities in the United States.

The summer of 2008 will see the film version of Mamma Mia!, with a screenplay by Catherine Johnson, reach cinemas across the globe with a star-studded cast which includes Meryl Streep as Donna, Julie Walters (Rosie), Amanda Seyfried (Sophie) and Dominic Cooper (Sky). Other great names include Colin Firth (Harry), Christine Baranski (Tanya) and Stellan Skarsgard (Bill) with Pierce Brosnan as Sam. Production on the movie began in the summer of 2007 directed by

BELOW Rehearsals in Hong Kong

Phyllida Lloyd while the production was headed up by Judy Craymer for Littlestar and Gary Goetzman for Playtone. The executive producers were Tom Hanks, Rita Wilson, Benny and Björn. Filming took place in London and Greece.

Although *Mamma Mia!* has been running since 1999, those involved are still striving to keep the show fresh. There is no sign, despite the thousands of performances across the globe that they are not achieving this, as their millions of eager audience members will testify. The film is surely bound to follow suit.

It has been announced that, at the end of 2008, the ABBA Museum will open in Stockholm. The custom-built museum will house the band members' former costumes, instruments, original sheet music, awards and other memorabilia as well as featuring a recording studio that allows visitors to participate in an interactive concert of their favourite songs at the touch of a button.

RIGHT
Benny, Frida and Björn
at the fifth anniversary
performance

The pictures in this book were provided courtesy of

GETTY IMAGES
www.gettyimages.com

Design and artwork by Jane Stephens

Image research by Jane Stephens

Creative Director: Kevin Gardner

Published by Green Umbrella Publishing

Publishers: Jules Gammond and Vanessa Gardner

Written by Claire Welch